'OXFORD COU

INCLUDING . . .

Burford, Bampton, Cumnor, Abington
Stanton St. John, Islip, Rousham, B|
The Tews, Charlbury, Woodstock, Ble

This guide book contains exact, bu ⌐ ⌐⌐⌐ motorist who wishes to combine visits to such well κιιυwn places as Woodstock, Burford or Abingdon, with an exploration of the small towns and villages of the Oxford countryside, that lie hidden beyond the network of busy main roads. A small area of Berkshire has been included to allow the route to "circumnavigate" Oxford without becoming entangled in its suburbs.

The 'Main Circle' route (Maps 1 – 15) shown on the Key Map opposite, covers 147 miles, most of which are through quiet country lanes. This route can be approached with ease from Oxford itself, or from Swindon, Cirencester, Stow-on-the-Wold, Stratford, Northampton, Aylesbury, High Wycombe or Reading. You will find that the strip maps show the 'A' roads approaching from the towns mentioned, thus giving you an easy link with 'civilization'.

The whole 15-map route is too long for a leisurely day's journey, and we would suggest that maps 9 – 10 – 11 – 12 – 13 would make a pleasant 'North Circle'. Maps 4 – 5 – 6 – 7 – 8 would make a good 'South Circle' and maps 14 – 15 – 1 – 2 – 3, a 'West Circle'. By using the Key Map opposite, you will soon find how easy it is to use short lengths of main roads as links between the strip maps.

HOW TO USE YOUR BOOK ON THE ROUTE

Each double page makes up a complete picture of the country ahead of you. On the left you will find a one inch to the mile strip map, with the route marked by a series of dashes. Direction is always from top to bottom, so that the map may be looked at in conjunction with the 'Directions for the Driver', with which it is cross referenced by a letter itemising each junction point. This enables the driver to have exact guidance every time an opportunity for changing direction occurs, even if it is only 'Keep straight, not left!'

With mileage intervals shown, the driver should even have warning when to expect these 'moments of decision', and if a signpost exists we have used this to help you, with the 'Follow Sign Marked . . .' column. However re-signing is always in progress, and this may lead to slight differences in sign marking in some cases . . . So beware of freshly erected signs.

We have also included a description of the towns and villages through which you will pass, together with some photographs to illustrate the route.

To gain full enjoyment from these journeys, be prepared to leave your car as often as possible. This will give you the opportunity, not only to look round castles, houses, parks and gardens, but also to wander at leisure amongst the quieter corners of this most modest Oxford countryside.

COMPILED BY PETER AND HELEN TITCHMARSH
PHOTOGRAPHY BY ALAN AND PETER TITCHMARSH

1

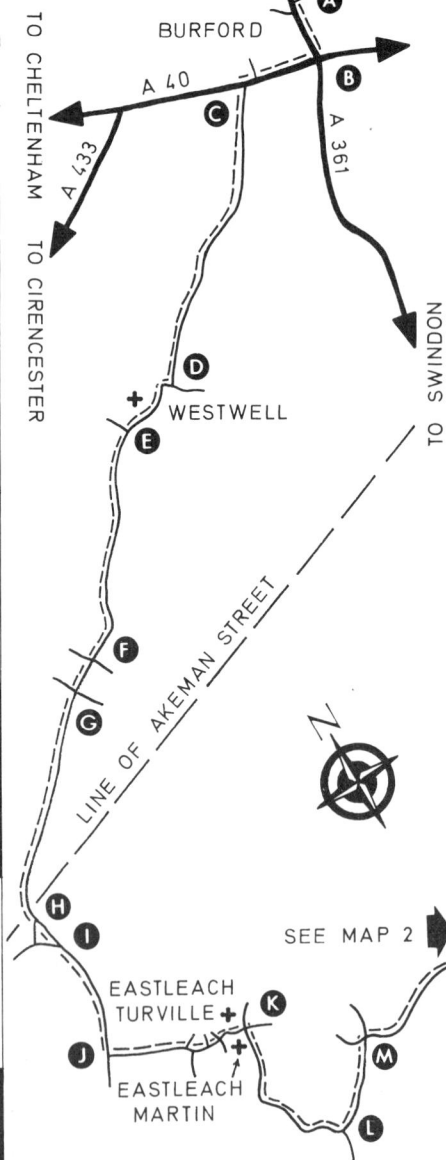

Map Reference	Miles	DIRECTIONS FOR DRIVER	FOLLOW SIGN MARKED
A		Leave Burford Centre, from the Tolsey Museum, and drive straight up High Street	No sign
B	.3	Turn right, on to A 40	Northleach
	.4	Straight, not right, keeping on A 40	No sign
C	.1	Turn left, off A 40	Westwell
D	1.7	Turn right at T junction at entry to Westwell	Westwell
	.1	Westwell duck-pond, war memorial and church on right	
E	.2	Straight, not right	No sign
F	1.3	Straight over X rds. with care	Eastleach Martin
		Fine views over towards the Berkshire Downs, on the left	
G	.4	Over small X rds.	Eastleach
	.9	Dip down into wide valley (River Leach), crossing the line of the Akeman Street	
H	.1	Fork left at Y junction	Eastleach
I	.2	Straight, not right	Eastleach
J	.7	Turn left at T junction	Eastleach
	.4	Bear right, keeping on lower road at entry to Eastleach	No sign
	.1	Bear left at X rds., just below Victoria Inn	Eastleach
	.1	Fork right down hill	Broadwell
	.1	Over small X rds. by war memorial, and...	No sign
		Into valley	
		Eastleach Turville church on left	
		Over Bridge crossing River Leach	
K	.1	Turn right at X rds. just beyond bridge	Southrop
		Eastleach Martin church on right	
L	.7	Bear left at T junction	Westwel
M	.5	Turn right at X rds.	Filkins
	.3	Enter Oxfordshire at 'Shire Gate', although no sign of a gate remains	
		Total mileage on this map: 8.9	

2

PLACES OF INTEREST ON THE ROUTE

Burford

Has an impressively wide main street dropping down from the wolds to the Windrush valley. The river is crossed by a fine medieval bridge, which has so far resisted the pressure of the highway improvers. The dignified church has a Norman tower capped with a slender 15th century spire. See the tombs of Sir Lawrence Tanfield, and Speaker Lenthall, the Member of Parliament who defied Charles 1st.

See also the Almshouses, the Grammar School, the little Tolsey Museum, and the 'Palladian' Methodist Chapel. However if you really wish to appreciate Burford, take time to walk the whole length of the High Street, and also take the quiet footpath westwards from the bridge along the banks of the Windrush.

1. *High Street, Burford*

Westwell

A delicious village with church, rectory and manor house looking out across a rough green, complete with pond. The impressively simple War Memorial incorporates a figure 'I', salvaged from the shattered Cloth Hall at Ypres. The Norman church stands amongst fascinating tombs, and from the south porch, a path leads towards the gorgeous rectory. Inside the church there is an attractive 17th century monument to the Trinder family, with husband, wife, six sons and eight daughters all depicted.

2. *The Rectory, Westwell*

Akeman Street

An important Roman road which ran from Cirencester to Bicester, and onwards to St. Albans. Unlike many Roman roads, it has not been retained as part of our main road network, although several sections have been used as minor roads, and a few as bridle-ways and footpaths. Immediately before Point H it is clearly visible as a terrace-way in the valley slopes on either side of our road.

3. *'Akeman Street Valley'*

Eastleach Turville and Eastleach Martin

The two parish churches solemnly regard each other across the little River Leach. Today Turville has the lion's share of the inhabitants, but Martin has the larger church. Both churches are however very pleasant and unspoilt buildings (see the Norman tympanum to Turville south doorway, and the 14th century transept at Martin).

Take time off to wander up the slopes of Turville, up past the war memorial, as far as the friendly little Victoria Inn, back down again, and across the little stone footbridge to Martin. If you pass this way in early spring you will be enchanted to find the banks of the Leach scattered with daffodils (but avoid weekends at this time if possible).

The road from Eastleach Martin to Southrop open to the River Leach in places and provides one or two lovely places for picnicking.

4. *Footbridge at Eastleach*

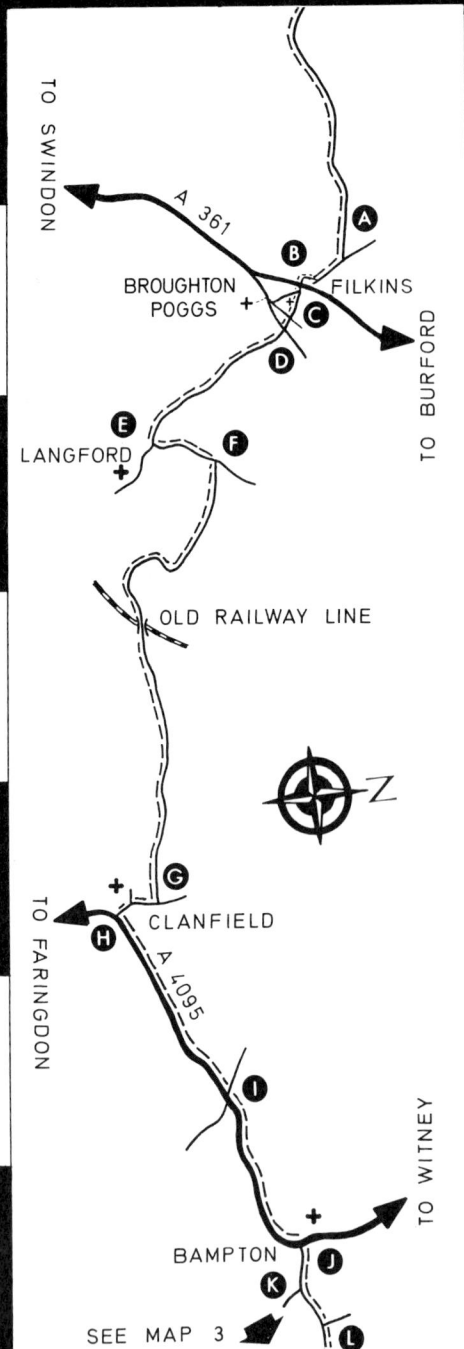

Map REFERENCE	Miles	DIRECTIONS FOR DRIVER	FOLLOW SIGN MARKE
A	1.2	Turn right at T junction	No sign
	.1	Turn right at T junction	Filkins
	.1	Under A 361, and.....	
		Enter Filkins	
B	.1	Fork left	No sign
		Filkins church on right	
C	.1	Over X rds. by the Lamb Inn	No sign
		(But turn right if you wish to visit Broughton Poggs church)	
D	.1	Over small X rds.	Langford
	.1	Fine row of poplars on right	
	.8	Enter Langford village	
E	.1	Turn left at T junction, by the Crown Inn. But keep straight if you wish to visit church, which is recommended	Broadwe
F	.4	Turn right at T junction	Clanfiel
	.9	Old water mill on right	
	.4	Cross deserted railway line	
G	1.6	Turn right at T junction	No sign
	.2	Enter Clanfield. Church on right up small cul-de-sac	
H	.1	Turn left just beyond the Plough Inn, on to A 4095	Bampton
I	1.1	Over offset X rds., keeping on A 4095	Bampton
	.5	Bampton entry signed	
		Keep into centre of town	
J	.4	Turn right by the Fire Station, onto the B 4449	Standlak
	.1	Keep straight by the New Inn, and follow out on B 4449	
K	.1	Bear left, keeping on B 4449	Standlak
		Total mileage on this map: 8.9	

4

PLACES OF INTEREST ON THE ROUTE

Filkins and Broughton Poggs

This is now virtually one long village, and all is happily by-passed by the busy A 361. Broughton Poggs church is a small Norman building with a squat saddle back tower, tucked away behind farm buildings (access via drive-way to Broughton Hall and not via farmyard). It has two small Norman doorways and a narrow Norman chancel arch.

Not far to the north is the cheerful Five Alls, an inn with a restaurant, and then beyond it, is Filkins church. This was designed by G.E. Street and is a pleasant 19th century building. We must admit however that our favourite building in Filkins is the Lamb Inn, splendidly clad in Virginia creeper. A small but interesting museum containing local byegones was established here many years ago by Sir Stafford and Lady Cripps.....ask locally for further details.

1. *The Post Office, Filkins*

Langford

A quiet village looking southwards towards flat Thames valley farmland, and the distant Berkshire Downs beyond. Langford's church is a little treasure house of medieval art and architecture and should not be missed. Built into the south porch, is a rare and beautiful Saxon carving of the Crucifixion and a 14th century carving with the figures of Mary and John. There are also other fascinating figures carved on the Norman tower. The Norman and Early English arches beneath the tower of this cruciform church are unusually lofty and on a sunny day one could imagine oneself to be in Provence rather than in Oxfordshire.

2. *The 11th Century Crucifix, Langford*

Clanfield

Long straggling village less than two miles north of the Thames, but still predominately Cotswold in flavour. It has two attractive inns, the Plough and the Mason's Arms, and a pretty stream beside the road.

The interior of the church is cold from over-restoration, but the exterior is well proportioned and is enlivened by a carving of St. Stephen high up on the 14th century tower, complete with the symbols of his martyrdom.....four stones.

Bampton

Once known as Bampton in the Bush, it is a quiet market town which has the good fortune to be miles from anywhere'. It has many pleasant 17th and 18th century houses, a few inns and a minute Town Hall, but its only building of outstanding interest is the church. This has a splendid 170 feet high spire, at whose base are four flying buttresses, each surmounted by a carved apostle. The contents of the interior include canopied sedilia in the chancel, a fine stone reredos, three brasses and an impressive 17th century monument (George Thomas, 1603).

3. *Bampton Church*

5

MAP **3**

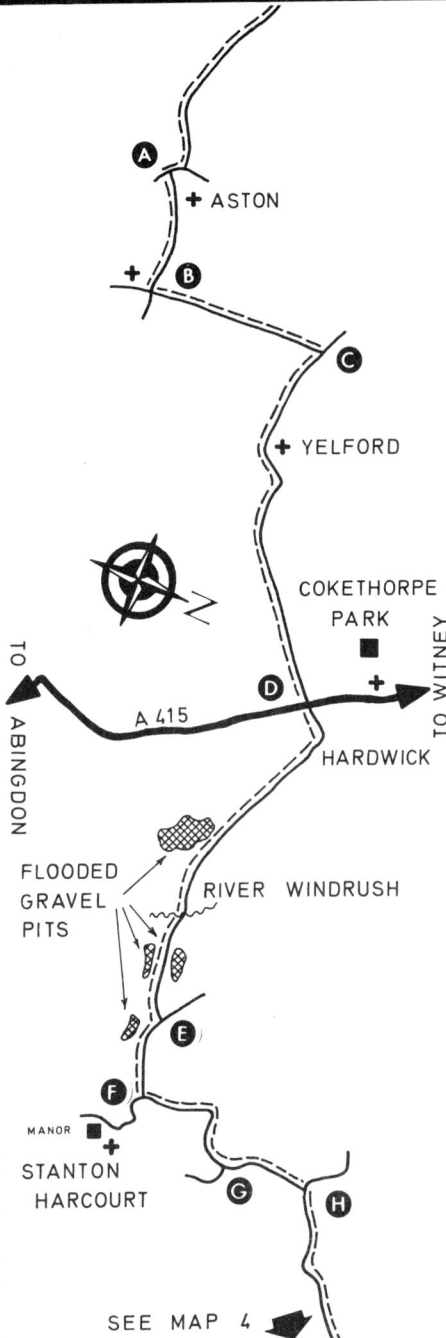

Map REFERENCE	Miles	DIRECTIONS FOR DRIVER	FOLLOW SIGN MARKE
	1.0	Enter Aston village	
A	.3	Bear right by the Red Lion, and immediately...	Cote
		Bear left, keeping on A 4449	Standlake
B	.7	Turn left at Cote Cross Roads	Yelford
C	1.0	Turn right at T junction	Yelford
	.7	Through Yelford. Tiny Church, almost hidden on left	
	.5	Fine views behind to the Berkshire Downs	
	.6	Cokethorpe Park just visible in trees to the left. Now a school	
D	.3	Over X rds., crossing A415. But turn left here if you wish to visit Cokethorpe Church	Hardwick
	.1	Enter Hardwick Hamlet	
	.8	Large gravel pit on right. Sailing and water ski-ing take place here	
	.5	Cross the River Windrush, about four miles above its confluence with the Thames	
E	.6	Straight, not left at entry to Stanton Harcourt	Stanton Harcourt
F	.5	Turn left at T junction, on to B 4449. But turn right to visit Stanton Harcourt village	Eynsham
	.2	Fox Inn on right	
G	.6	Straight, not right	No sign
H	.5	Bear right at T junction	No sign
		Total mileage on this map: 8.9	

Map labels: ASTON, YELFORD, COKETHORPE PARK, TO WITNEY, A 415, TO ABINGDON, HARDWICK, FLOODED GRAVEL PITS, RIVER WINDRUSH, MANOR, STANTON HARCOURT, SEE MAP 4

Aston

The Victorian church (1839) is remarkably unfussy in design, but apart from this and the Red Lion, Aston contains little of interest.

Cote

This hamlet contains one of the earliest Baptist Chapels in the country (1664). Turn right at junction B, to look at this oddly attractive building. Further down this road, in the Thames meadowlands, is 17th century Cote House, a glimpse of which may be taken through beautiful wrought iron gates.

1. *The Red Lion, Aston*

Yelford

Consists of a minute church, one or two cottages, and the manor farmhouse amongst the trees. This was the home of Warren Hastings' distant ancestors before the family moved to Daylesford, near Stow-on-the-Wold. The church is not as beautiful as its setting, but the porch is attractive.

2. *Yelford Church*

Cokethorpe Park

This dignified 18th century mansion (now a school) was built by the 1st Lord Harcourt, Lord Chancellor in Queen Anne's reign. The house is set in a magnificent park, across part of which one can walk to visit the church, a small 15th century building which has a worthwhile Norman font, but little else of interest.

3. *Cokethorpe Park*

Stanton Harcourt

A most attractive village containing the remains of a mansion, built by the Harcourts in the 15th century, vacated by them in the 18th century, and now partly restored.

The parts remaining include: (1) Popes Tower, close to the church, where Alexander Pope spent two summers working on his transmission of Homer, (2) An intriguing medieval kitchen, with a conical roof, topped by a griffin. Both these buildings stand in the restored manor's delicious garden, which includes a lovely tree shaded lake. This garden may be open about twice a year. (See National Gardens Scheme booklet, published annually.)

The cruciform church is partly Norman and has a fine 15th century roof, and a splendid oak chancel screen with many interesting carved details. However the outstanding feature here is the Harcourt Chapel with its series of magnificent Harcourt monuments.....emphasising the importance of this ancient family at several stages of our history.

4. *Stanton Harcourt Church*

7

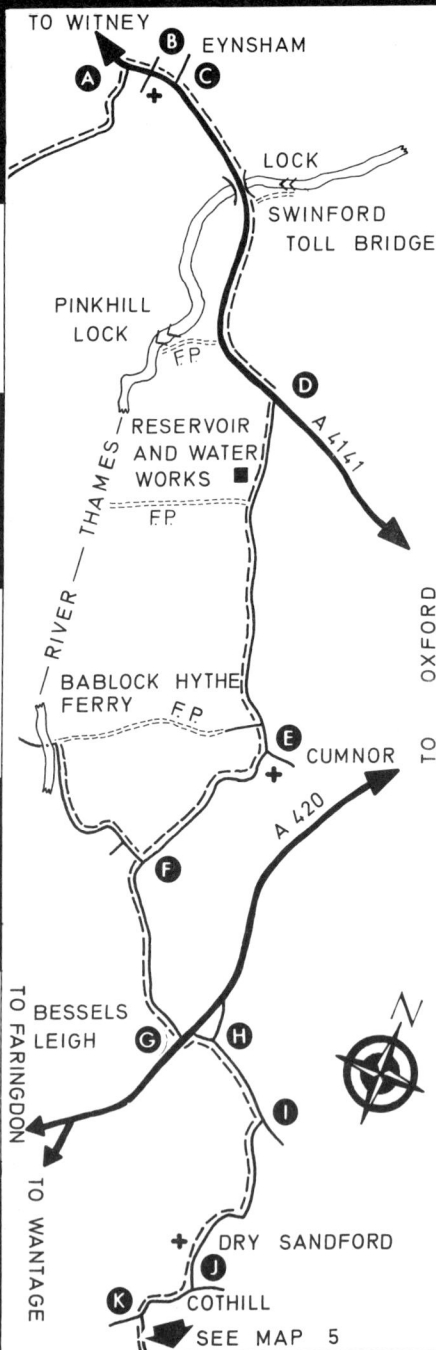

MAP 4

Map Reference	Miles	Directions for Driver	Follow Sign Marked
	1.3	Enter Eynsham	
A	.4	Turn right at T junction on to A 4141	Oxford
B	.1	Over X rds. by village lock-up	No sign
C	.2	Straight, not left	Oxford
	.4	Talbot Inn on left	
	.2	Cross River Thames by the Swinford Toll Bridge and enter Berkshire	
	.9	Footpath on right to Pinkhill Lock	
	.2	Through Farmoor	
D	.2	Turn right, on to B 4017	Cumnor
	.3	Large reservoir on right	
	.1	Footpath on right, ⋯ beside reservoir. Sailing visible	
	1.4	Enter Cumnor	
		Footpath on right, to Bablock Hythe Ferry	
E	.2	Turn sharp right	'Appleton Road'
		(But bear left if you wish to visit church)	
F	1.0	Straight, not right	Bessel's Leigh
		(But turn right if you wish to visit Bablock Hythe Ferry)	
	.8	Enter Bessel's Leigh hamlet	
G	.3	Turn left on to A 420 by the Grey Hound Inn	No sign
		Immediately turn right on to B 4017	Abingdon
H	.1	Turn right again at T junction	Wootton
I	.6	Turn right at T junction	Dry Sandford
	.8	Enter Dry Sandford	
J	.4	Turn right at T junction	Cothill
	.2	Fleur de Lys Inn on left	
K	.1	Fork left	Shippon
		Total mileage on this map: 10.2	

8

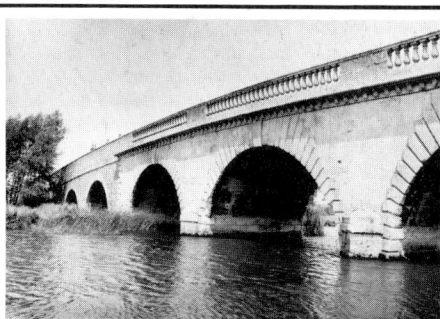

1. *Swinford Bridge*

Eynsham

There are several pleasant houses and inns in this quiet little town, and in the market square there is an emaciated, iron-bound cross. Opposite the cross is Eynsham church, with many excellent Perpendicular features, including a solid tower and a north porch with a priest's chamber above.

In the fields beyond the church, the Anglo-Saxons built a Benedictine monastery but although this grew to be an important establishment in the Middle Ages, no trace now remains.

Swinford Bridge

Walk down to the tow-path to appreciate the quality of this splendid 18th century bridge. Tolls are still charged here, as the bridge is privately owned, but who shall begrudge a few pence for the descendants of a man who commissioned this excellent design. Walk a few yards downstream to Swinford Lock, or a mile and a half upstream to Pinkhill, for it is always a pleasure to stand in the sun and watch a boat or two being 'locked through' on their way to Godstow, Bablock Hythe or Tadpole Bridge.

2. *Pinkhill Lock, River Thames*

Farmoor Reservoir

There is a pleasant walk to the Thames, beside this large reservoir (see Route Directions, beyond Point D).

Cumnor

Cumnor Place, the house where Amy Robsart (wife of Robert Dudley, later Earl of Leicester) met her mysterious death in 1560, was demolished in the 19th century. However the tomb of its owner, and possible murderer of Amy, Anthony Forster, is to be found in Cumnor church. This fine building has a squat Norman tower, and contains some exceptional woodwork, including a magnificent 17th century spiral staircase to the belfry and a large two-decker pulpit of the same period.

Note also the attractive, 17th century Bear and Ragged Staff Inn.

3. *Cumnor Church*

Bablock Hythe Ferry

May be reached on foot, by turning right immediately on entering Cumnor (.2 miles before junction E), or by car, by turning right at junction F. However avoid it on a summer Sunday, when outboard motors and transistors overwhelm Matthew Arnold's much quoted 'stripling Thames'.

Dry Sandford and Cothill

Oxford dormitory area with only a few houses of character in evidence.

4. *The Greyhound, Bessels Leigh*

MAP 5

MILES

TO FARINGDON

A 415

A 34

TO NEWBURY

M.G. WORKS

TO OXFORD

ABINGDON

RIVER THAMES A 415

DRAYTON

SUTTON COURTENAY

APPLETON

DIDCOT ATOMIC POWER STATION

TO DORCHESTER

N

SEE MAP 6

KILOMETRES

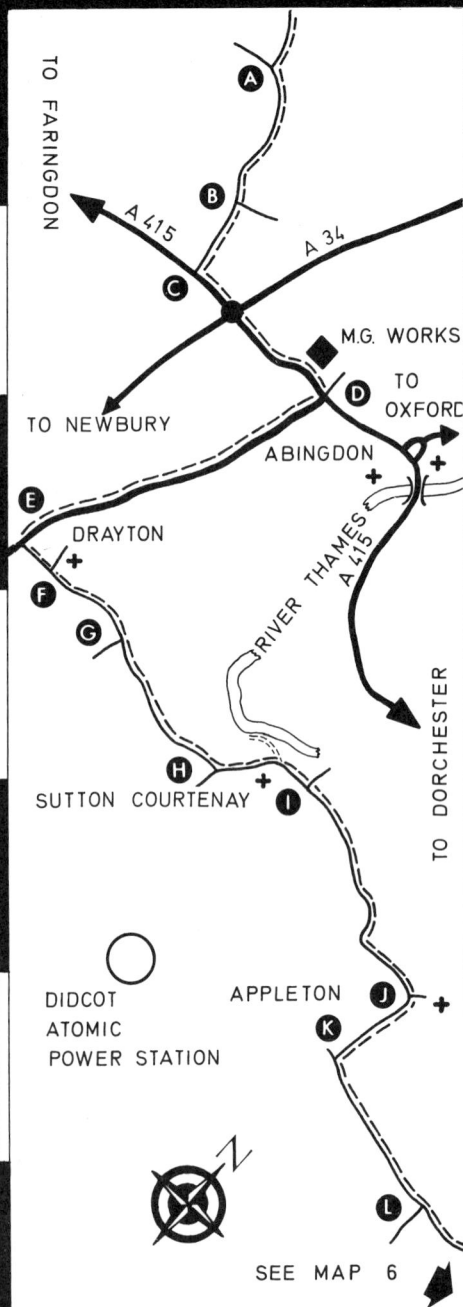

Map REFERENCE	Miles	DIRECTIONS FOR DRIVER	FOLLOW SIGN MARKED
A	.6	Turn left at T junction	Abingdon
B	.8	Straight, not left	Abingdon
C	.4	Turn left, on to A 415	Abingdon
	.3	Go straight under A 34, at intersection	Abingdon
	.3	Enter Abingdon	
	.2	M.G. Car Factory on left	
D	.2	Turn right at small roundabout	Drayton
		(But go straight ahead if you wish to visit Abingdon)	
		Leave Abingdon on main road	
	1.4	Enter Drayton	
	.4	Red Lion on right	
E	.1	Turn left on to B 4016	Sutton Courtenay
F	.2	Straight, not left	No sign
		(But turn left if you wish to visit church)	
	.1	Fine Manor House on right	
G	.4	Straight, not right	Sutton Courtenay
	.7	Sutton Courtenay entry signed	
H	.2	Bear left at T junction	Culham
	.2	Church on right, Manor House on left	
	.1	Footpath to Thames at corner on left	
I	.3	Straight, not left	Appleford
	.5	Didcot Nuclear Power Station up right	
J	.6	Bear right in Appleford	Didcot
K	.6	Bear left by level-crossing	No sign
L	.9	Straight, not right	Long Wittenham
		Sinodun Hills visible ahead	
		Total mileage on this map: 9.5	

PLACES OF INTEREST ON THE ROUTE

Abingdon

Abingdon grew up around its famous Abbey, which was founded in 676, sacked by the Danes, and then re-founded in 955. By the time of the Abbey's dissolution, the town's important bridge across the Thames, coupled with its considerable trade in wool, resulted in continuing prosperity.

Today it remains a lively and colourful town, and its charms have recently been greatly enhanced by the building of a by-pass, which has removed the A 34's traffic well away to the west. It has many interesting corners to explore, but we would especially recommend the following:

1) The *Abbey Gate House,* the *Long Gallery* and the *Chequer*.....all that remain of the great Abbey.
2) *St. John's Hospital Chapel,* which became the Borough Court, together with the fine 18th century Council Chamber.
3) The *Town Hall,* built in the late 17th century, by Christopher Kempster of Burford, one of Christopher Wren's master masons. This splendid building is without doubt one of the finest specimens in the country.
4) *St. Helen's Church,* with its 13th century spire, and its magnificent 14th century painted roof over the north aisle.
5) The wonderful *Almshouses* around three sides of St. Helen's churchyard.....the oldest of the three ranges having been built as early as 1446.
6) The walks along both banks of the Thames, with the well restored bridge and St. Helen's spire, both overlooking the comings and goings of colourful pleasure boats.

1. *The Town Hall, Abingdon*

2. *The Thames, Abingdon*

3. *Sutton Courtenay Church*

Drayton

Once away from the still busy main road, Drayton assumes a pleasant relaxed air, with several interesting old houses, now mostly in attractive mellow brick. The lovely manor house, is especially worthwhile. The church was heavily restored in the 19th century, but enthusiasts should not miss the very fine 15th century reredos, or altar-piece.

Sutton Courtenay

A dream of a village, whose wide greens, and luxuriant trees warrant a hot summer afternoon. Beyond the Swan Inn lies an attractive Norman towered church. Opposite to the church, are the Manor House, and the 'Norman Hall', both of which date back to the medieval period. The Victorian front of the 'Abbey' (opposite junction H), conceals a 14th century grange.

At the far end of the village, a path leads to Sutton Pool, a delightful Thames backwater. Walk down here, but beware of "Sunday crowding".

4. *Sutton Courtenay*

11

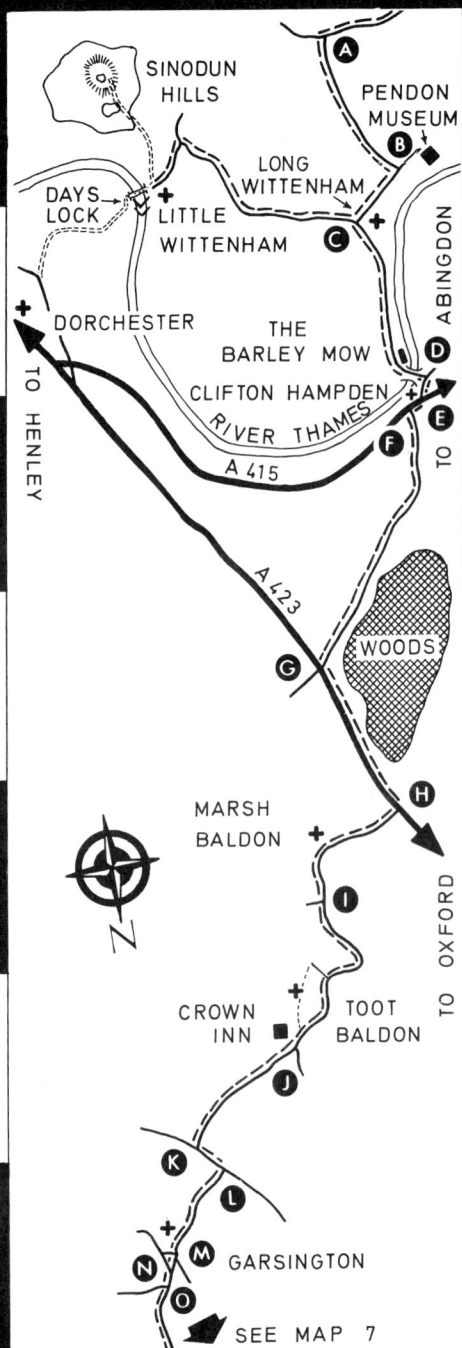

Map REFERENCE	Miles	DIRECTIONS FOR DRIVER	FOLLOW SIGN MARKED
A	.7	Bear left at T junction	Long Wittenham
	.7	Enter Long Wittenham	
B	.2	Turn right at T junction (But turn right if you wish to visit the Pendon Museum, on right at end of cul-de- sac)	Clifton Hampden
	.2	Church down to left	
C	.1	Fork left (But fork right to visit Little Wittenham, which is 1¼ miles ahead)	Clifton Hampden
	.4	Thames now close to left of road. Picnic possibilities	
	.4	Barley Mow Inn on left	
	.1	Cross Thames into Oxfordshire at Clifton Hampden	
D	.1	Bear right after crossing bridge	No sign
E	.1	Turn right on to A 415	Dorchester
F	.1	Almost immediately turn left on to B 4015 (But go straight ahead for 3 miles if you wish to visit Dorchester)	Oxford
	.9	Woods on left	
G	.6	Turn left, and bear left, on to A 423	Oxford
	.7	Entrance to Nuneham Park on left	
H	.2	Turn right at T junction off A 423	'The Baldons'
	.5	Enter Marsh Baldon	
	.1	Seven Stars Inn and attractive, large village green on right	
I	.2	Straight, not right, at end of green	No sign
	.7	Straight, not right, at entry to Toot Baldon	No sign
	.4	Drive-way to church on right, and.....	
J		Fork right by the Crown Inn	No sign
K	.9	Turn left on to B 480	Cowley
L	.1	Turn right at T junction	Garsington
	.3	Up hill into Garsington	
M	.2	Over X rds. by the Plough Inn	Wheatley
N	.1	Straight, not right	Wheatley
O	.1	Straight not right	Wheatley
		Total mileage on this map: 9.2	

PLACES OF INTEREST ON THE ROUTE

1. *Long Wittenham*

Long Wittenham

The church, the path to which lies alongside an attractive half-timbered farmhouse, has many Norman features, including a fine chancel arch with beasts carved on one of the capitals. See also the charming piscina, with angels hovering over a tiny recumbent knight, and the Norman lead font.

At the other end of the village, is the Pendon Museum, where a team of craftsmen are building up a series of intricate and highly detailed models of the English countryside. The main scenes are the Vale of White Horse, the western fringes of Dartmoor, and the 'Nadder Valley' a fictional harbour town. There is also an interesting collection of early railway relics. Do not miss a visit to this unique display.

Little Wittenham

The short diversion is amply justified by the walk down past the little church, to Day's Lock. If the day is fine, walk on across the meadows to Dorchester, which lies about a mile away.

Sinodun Hills

Walk up from Little Wittenham to explore the Iron Age earthworks, and to enjoy the splendid prospect of the Oxfordshire and Berkshire countryside. The two hills were known locally as the Berkshire Bubs, or Mother Dunch's Buttocks. The Dunches were squires of Little Wittenham for two centuries, but apparently failed to earn universal respect!

2. *The Thames at Little Wittenham*

Clifton Hampden

The charming black and white, Barley Mow Inn, immortalised in 'Three Men in a Boat', stands on the Berkshire side of Clifton Hampden Bridge. This excellent mellow brick, six arched bridge, was built by Sir Gilbert Scott in 1864, and is overlooked by the little church, from its rocky bluff on the Oxfordshire side of the curving river. Add a few boats and children paddling in the shallows, and you have the classic Thames-side scene.....very satisfying.

Marsh Baldon

Consists of picturesque cottages scattered round an immense green, complete with cricket pitch, willow bordered stream, and a small inn. The church has a Jacobean pulpit, and some interesting stained glass.

3. *The Thames from Clifton Hampden Bridge*

Toot Baldon

A quiet village with thatched cottages, an inn, and a small church pleasantly sited on slopes well to the south of our road. It has the base of a 15th century cross in the churchyard, and a little bellcote at its west end. The interior contains well sculptured arcade capitals, but little else of interest to visitors.

Garsington

Hill top village, with a church that looks across the Thames valley to the Chilterns and the Berkshire Downs. Do not miss the small brass of Thomas Ridley with his wife and children, nor the interesting corbel figures supporting the nave roof.

4. *Garsington Church*

MAP 7

MILES

KILOMETRES

TO HIGH WYCOMBE

WHEATLEY

A 40

N

FOREST HILL

STANTON ST. JOHN

T.V. MAST

BECKLEY

TO OXFORD

SEE MAP 8

Map REFERENCE	Miles	DIRECTIONS FOR DRIVER	FOLLOW SIGN MARKED
A	1.4	Straight, not left	Wheatley
B	.3	Straight, not right	Wheatley
	.4	Enter Wheatley, and.....	
		Down hill	
C	.3	Bear left near bottom of hill	No sign
D	.1	Turn left at X rds., into High Street	'High Street'
	.2	Turn right at small X rds by Lautrec Cottage, into Church Road	'Church Road'
E	.1	Turn left just beyond Pyramid 'Lock-up' on left	Holton
F	.1	Bear left, and.....	Oxford
G	.1	Keep left, and join A40 with great care	No sign
H	.3	Turn right with great care, on to B 4027	Forest Hill
	.7	Enter Forest Hill	
I	.3	Turn right by the King's Arms	Stanton St. John
J	.8	Turn right immediately before George Inn, and.....	No sign
		Enter Stanton St. John	
K	.2	Fork left	No sign
L	.1	Straight, not left	No sign
M	.1	Fork left beyond the church	Oxford
N	.3	Turn right on to B 4027	Islip
O	.1	Straight, not left	Islip
P	.4	Over X rds.	Islip
Q	.1	Fork right	Beckley
	.1	Beckley T.V. Transmitter on right	
	.5	Fine views of Otmoor on right	
R	.2	Turn left, but go straight to visit Beckley village	No sign
S	.8	Turn right, re-joining B 4027	No sign
		Keep on B 4027 for 7½ miles until reaching the Rock of Gibraltar Inn (Map 8, Junction J)	
		Total mileage on this map: 8.0	

14

PLACES OF INTEREST ON THE ROUTE

Wheatley

Mercifully, just clear of the London road, Wheatley is a large village, with a leisurely air. The 19th century church is by G.E. Street, one of our favourite Victorians (see Filkins, page 5), and there are several pleasant stone houses and inns. Opinions as to the age of the unusual 'Pyramid' lock-up are divided, but it is probably late 18th or early 19th century

1. Pyramid Lock-up Wheatley

2. Door of John White's House, Stanton St. John

Forest Hill

Not a village of any special charm, although its church (straight, not right at junction I) was the scene of the poet Milton's first marriage. This was to 17 year old Mary Powell, daughter of a Forest Hill landowner, in the year 1643.

The church, which was restored by Sir Gilbert Scott, has a fine Norman chancel arch and an unusually large west bellcote.

3. Stanton St. John Church

Stanton St. John

Pleasant stone built village, once the home of Milton's ancestors, looking eastwards towards the great woodlands of Stanton, Waterperry and Holton. Being in the possession of Eynsham Abbey at the time of the dissolution, the church and much other property in Stanton St. John was sold to New College, Oxford for the princely sum of £22.4.2.

The church bears evidence of the care bestowed upon it by New College over the centuries. There is some fine 14th century glass, richly carved window mouldings incorporating the heads of kings and bishops, and some excellent examples of wood carving on pulpit, reading desk and pew ends. Do not miss this exceptionally interesting church, and before leaving read the inscription over the door of the house opposite.....the birthplace of John White, chief founder of the Colony of Massachusetts.

4. Cottages at Beckley

Beckley

Quiet village on a hillside overlooking the lonely expanse of Otmoor, and the wooded hills beyond. Beckley has a friendly inn, many thatched stone cottages, and a church full of atmosphere. See especially the wide medieval south door with its splendid ironwork, the Jacobean pulpit, and the beautiful 14th century glass.

5. Prospect of Otmoor

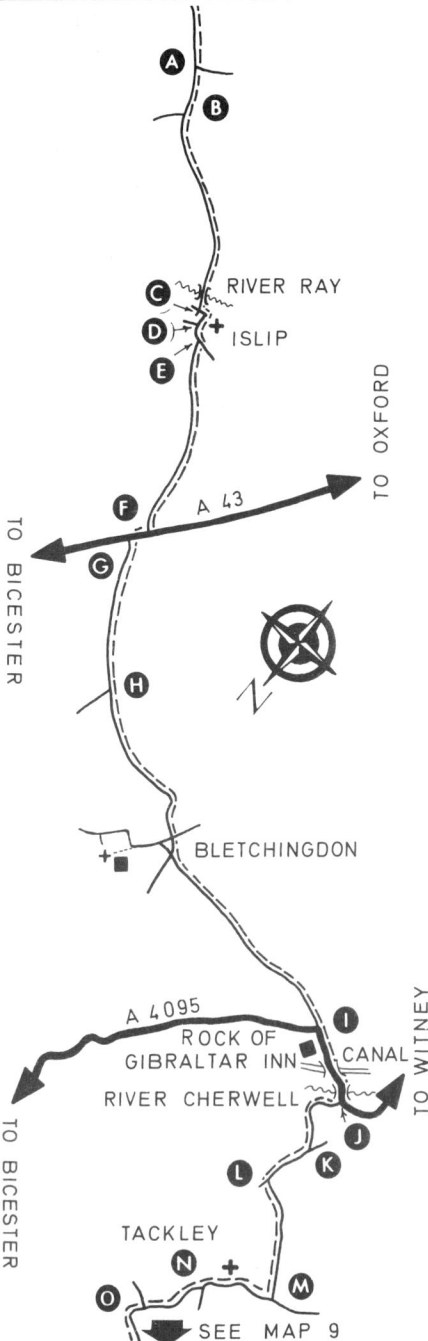

MAP 8

RIVER RAY

ISLIP

TO OXFORD

TO BICESTER

A 43

N

BLETCHINGDON

A 4095

ROCK OF
GIBRALTAR INN   CANAL

RIVER CHERWELL

TO WITNEY

TO BICESTER

TACKLEY

SEE MAP 9

CROWN COPYRIGHT RESERVED

Map REFERENCE	Miles	DIRECTIONS FOR DRIVER	FOLLOW SIGN MARKED
A	1.4	Straight, not left	No sign
B	.3	Straight, not right	No sign
	.9	Islip entry signed	
	.1	Cross River Ray	
C	.1	Bear left beyond bridge and almost immediately turn right	Bletchingdon Oxford
D	.1	Straight, not right, by the church	No sign
		Follow out of village on B 4027	
E	.1	Fork right by war memorial	Bletchingdon
F	1.1	Turn right on to A 43	Bicester
G		Immediately turn left on on to B 4027	Bletchingdon
H	.9	Straight, not right	Bletchingdon
		Wide verges beyond, with picnic possibilities	
	.6	Bletchingdon entry signed	
	.2	Straight, not right twice, by green (But turn right if you wish to visit church — .5)	No sign
		Black Boy Inn on left	
	.1	Straight, not right, at end of village	No sign
	.8	Dropping down into Cherwell valley	
I	.5	Straight, not right	Woodstock
	.2	The Rock of Gibraltar Inn on right	
		Over Oxford Canal	
	.2	Over River Cherwell	
J	.1	Immediately turn sharp right at end of bridge (WATCH FOR THIS WITH CARE)	No sign
K	.4	Turn right at T junction	No sign
L	.4	Bear left	No sign
M	.7	Turn right at T junction	No sign
	.1	Tackley entry signed	
N	.3	Keep right at village green	No sign
O	.4	Straight, not right	Steeple Ast
		Total mileage on this map: 10.0	

16

PLACES OF INTEREST ON THE ROUTE

Islip

Attractively sited on the banks of the little river Ray, which is crossed here by a fine stone bridge; scene of several skirmishes in the Civil War. Islip's charm is further enhanced by several tall poplars along the banks of the stream, and the pleasant Perpendicular church tower rising above it all. The church deserves a visit, although its over-restored interior is in startling contrast to delightful Beckley.

Edward the Confessor, who was born in Islip, at a hunting lodge of the Saxon kings, gave Islip to Westminster Abbey, and this link was maintained until the late 19th century.

Bletchingdon

Dignified stone built village set around a large tree bordered green. The inn is amusingly titled 'The Black Boy', and has been well restored.

The church lies beyond the northern end of the village, in a delightful setting amidst trees, within the confines of Bletchingdon Park. It has a pleasant Perpendicular tower, but its interior has been over-restored. Faith Coghill, the wife of Christopher Wren, came from a Bletchingdon family, and there are three handsome Coghill wall monuments in the chancel.

Bletchingdon Park, a fine classical mansion is visible from one side of the churchyard, and on the other there is a massive range of stable buildings topped with a pretty little cupola.

Oxford Canal

Running 77 miles from Hawkesbury Junction to Oxford, it was completed in 1790 by James Brindley, thus allowing coal from the Coventry pits to be shipped down the Thames. Try the lovely towpath walk to Hampton Gay (2 miles south).

Tackley

The wide green is overlooked by pleasant, trim stone houses, and a restored 16th century gateway. Everything in Tackley is almost too tidy, but the little 'Gardiner Arms' still looks full of character.

The church looks out over the village to the Cherwell valley, and as at Islip, poplars enliven the scene. Venture into the rather gloomy church to see the charming 17th century monument of John Harbourne, his wife and their many children. The two 18th century monuments by John Bacon, in complete contrast, display an elegance unknown to the earlier sculptor, but lack his sense of involvement.

1. *Islip Bridge*

2. *The Rock of Gibralter*

3. *Tackley, from the churchyard.*

17

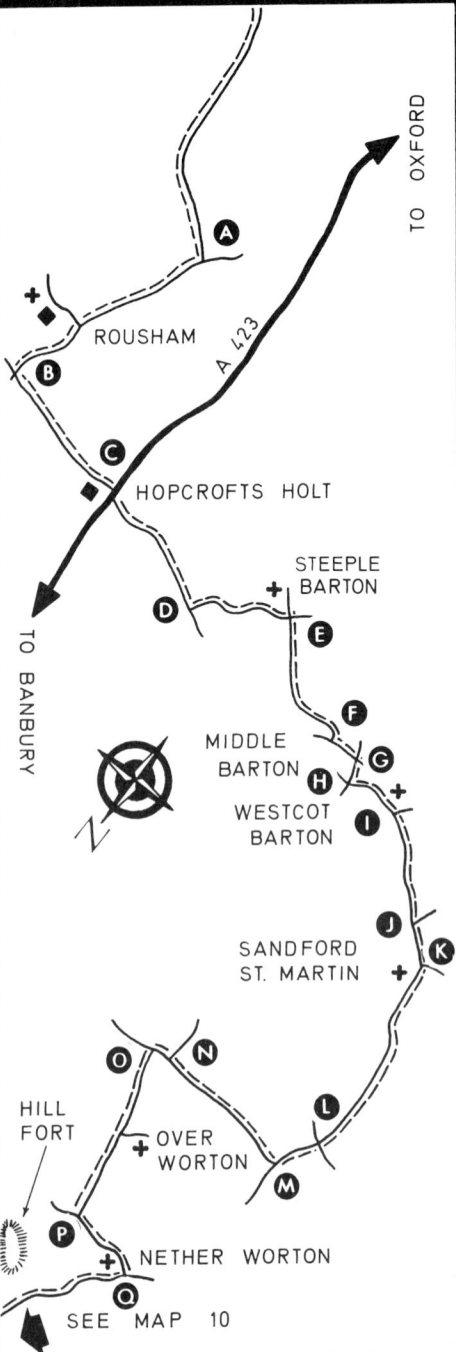

MAP 9

MILES / KILOMETRES

TO OXFORD

TO BANBURY

ROUSHAM

A 423

HOPCROFTS HOLT

STEEPLE BARTON

MIDDLE BARTON

WESTCOT BARTON

SANDFORD ST. MARTIN

HILL FORT

OVER WORTON

NETHER WORTON

SEE MAP 10

N

Map REFERENCE	Miles	DIRECTIONS FOR DRIVER	FOLLOW SIGN MARKED
A	1.7	Turn right at T junction	No sign
	.5	Enter Rousham	
	.3	Entrance to Rousham Park on right. Access to church and village also	
B	.4	Turn left at X rds. on to B 4030	Barton
C	.8	Over X rds. crossing A 423, by Hopcroft's Holt Hotel	'The Bartons'
	.7	Gates of Barton Abbey on left	
D	.1	Turn left at T junction	Steeple Barton
	.5	Enter Steeple Barton	
E	.2	Turn right at small X rds. (But turn left to visit church)	Middle Barton
	.6	Enter Middle Barton	
F	.1	Turn left at T junction	No sign
G	.2	Turn right at small X rds.	No sign
H	.1	Turn left on B 4030	Enstone
	.2	Westcot Barton church on left	
I	.1	Fork right, off B 4030	Sandford St. Martin
J	.6	Straight, not left	Sandford
	.1	Enter Sandford St. Martin	
K	.1	Fork right by the War Memorial	No sign
L	1.2	Over X rds.	Nether Worton
M	.3	Turn right at T junction	Over Worton
N	.9	Straight, not right	Worton
O	.1	Turn left at T junction	Over Worton
	.3	Pass through Over Worton hamlet. (But turn left to visit church)	
	.2	Church just visible away on left	
P	.4	Turn left at T junction on edge of unfenced field	No sign
	.4	Nether Worton church on right	
Q	.1	Turn right at T junction Manor House on left	Barford
	.4	Iron Age Hill Fort visible on right	
		Total mileage on this map: 11.6	

PLACES OF INTEREST ON THE ROUTE

1. *Rousham House*

Rousham

Jacobean mansion enlarged and enriched by William Kent in 1738. While the house with its fine collection of portraits and furniture is of considerable interest, a visit to its landscape gardens is a unique experience.

The only surviving example of Kent's landscape design, Rousham Gardens are sited along the rushy, tree shaded banks of the Cherwell. Walking amongst these hanging woods, one comes across Italian Statuary, sparkling rivulets, and a lovely Classical summer house, from whence one can look out across the valley.

See also the lovely old flower borders in the walled garden, the 16th century dovecot with revolving ladder, and the church, with its Cottrell-Dormer monuments.

Hopcroft's Holt

A comfortable looking wayside hotel where legends of highwaymen persist. But the sordid truth points to the murder of the inn keeper and his wife by a petty thief, one night in January 1754.....so much for the 'gentlemen of the road'!

2. *Hopcroft's Holt*

Steeple Barton

A beautifully quiet place with a few houses and a church standing by itself at the end of a lane. There is no sign of a steeple here, but the stout Perpendicular tower dominates the large sloping churchyard. The interior contains arcading ornamented with splendid medieval heads of both men and beasts.

Middle and Westcot Barton

The character of Middle Barton has been much altered by modern building. However, do look at the 15th century chancel screen in Westcot Barton church.

Sandford St. Martin

Delightful stone built village, with a fine manor house and a lovely 18th century mansion opposite the church. Lord Deloraine, third son of the ill fated Duke of Monmouth, is buried in the churchyard.

3. *The road near Nether Worton*

Over Worton

There is a delightful open road between here and Nether Worton, overlooked by a Victorian church beautifully situated in a clump of trees. To reach the church, walk in front of the dignified late Georgian manor. The church has no special features of interest, but do not overlook the beautiful little Georgian rectory beyond the churchyard path.

Nether Worton

An immaculate farm, a very grand manor house, and a minute church, with deserted schoolroom attached. This and a few cottages make up Nether Worton, a deliciously quiet hamlet sheltering beneath wooded Hawk Hill.

4. *Nether Worton Church*

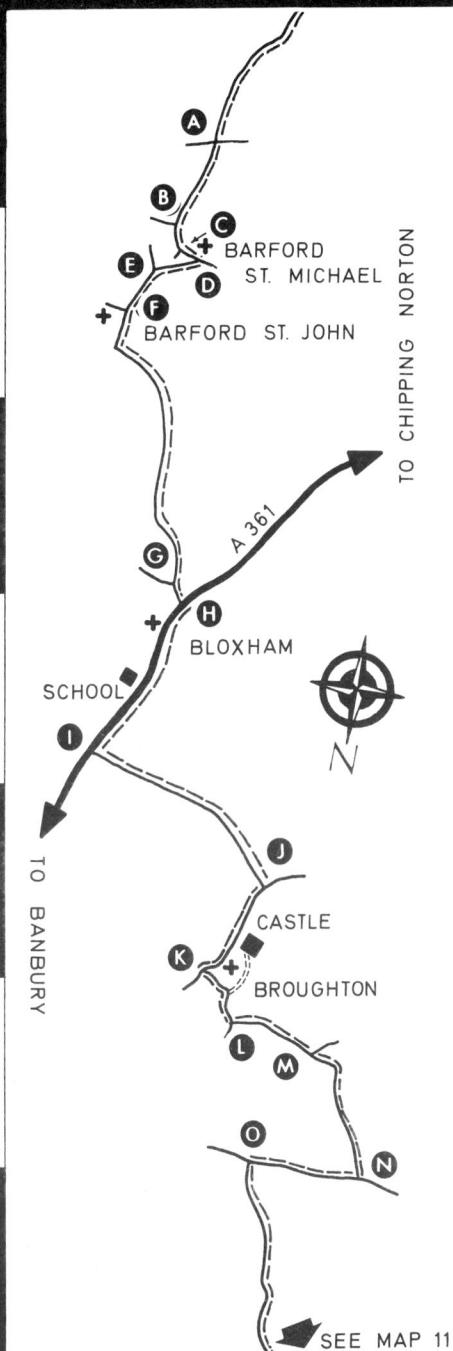

Map REFERENCE	Miles	DIRECTIONS FOR DRIVER	FOLLOW SIGN MARKED
A	.7	Over X rds., crossing B 4031	Barfords
B	.5	Straight, not right	South Newington
C	.1	Fork left at entry to Barford St. Michael	No sign
D	.1	Turn right beyond church	'Lower Street'
E	.3	Turn left at T junction	No sign
		Cross River Swere	
	.2	Enter Barford St. John	
F	.1	Straight, not right (But turn right to visit the church)	No sign
	.3	Large Radio Station on right	
	1.2	Enter Bloxham	
G	.1	Straight, not right	Bloxham
H	.1	Turn right on to A 361	Banbury
	.5	Bloxham School on right	
		Leave Bloxham on A 361	
I	.5	Turn left at T junction	Tadmartor
J	1.2	Turn right at T junction on to B 4035	Broughton
	.2	Cross River Soar at entrance to Broughton	
	.1	Broughton Castle on left (But entrance ½ mile onwards)	
K	.3	Turn left at small X rds. by the Saye and Sele Arms	Broughton Castle
	.2	Entrance to Broughton Castle on left	
L	.1	Fork left	Shutford
		Picnic possibilities here	
M	.5	Fork right, not left to Fulling Mill	No sign
N	.7	Turn right at T junction beyond gate	No sign
O	.6	Turn left at T junction	Wroxton
		Total mileage on this map: 7.6	

PLACES OF INTEREST ON THE ROUTE

1. *Norman Doorway, Barford St. Michael*

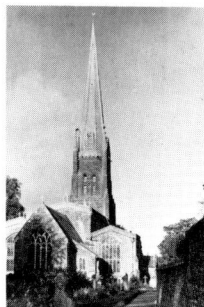

2. *Bloxham Church*

Barford St. Michael

A stone and thatch village looking out over the Swere valley, with a pleasant little thatched inn called the George, and considerable modern development at its southern end. The squat towered Norman church stands well above our road, with quiet views from its Norman north doorway. This is one of Oxfordshire's outstanding art treasures, with fantastic carvings of beak heads and chevrons, and intertwining decoration on capitals and tympanum. Please spare time to look at this magnificent work.

Barford St. John

Faces Barford St. Michael across the river Swere. Its little church lies behind a farmyard, and although heavily restored, it possesses a good Norman doorway.

Bloxham

A large village strung out along the A 361, Bloxham has a strong enough character to overcome this disadvantage. Its well built stone houses, cottages and inns are sited on a multitude of different levels.

3. *The George Inn, Barford St. Michael*

At the Banbury end of the village, stands Bloxham School, most of which was designed by G.E. Street (see Filkins, page 5). However the focal point of Bloxham is its magnificent 14th century church spire, which soars to a height of almost 200 feet. The church below is of considerable scale, and is well worth visiting, It has an attractive south doorway, and some fascinating medieval stone figures, beneath the tower parapet, and high up in the north aisle. See also the very grand 18th century tomb to Sir John Thorneycroft.

Broughton

Built in 1306, Broughton Castle is the home of Lord Saye and Sele, whose ancestor, the second Baron acquired it by marriage to the heiress of William of Wykeham, founder of Winchester and New College, Oxford. In the 16th century a beautiful 'Elizabethan' front was added and, many interior improvements carried out, but this has not disturbed Broughton's extraordinarily strong atmosphere. Viewed from the park across its reedy moat, the castle reveals itself as one of Oxfordshire's most romantic. buildings.

4. *Broughton Castle*

The tall spired church sits between the edge of Broughton Castle's park and the small stream which feeds the castle's moat. It is a pleasant building with fine old roofs, an interesting 14th century stone chancel screen, and a splendid series of monuments. See especially those of Thomas Broughton (the original builder of the castle), and of Sir Thomas Wykeham and his wife.

5. *The Gatehouse, Broughton Castle.*

TO STRATFORD
A 422
① = TO BANBURY
② = TO WROXTON
BALSCOTT
SHUTFORD
MADMARSTON HILL
LINE OF ROMAN ROAD
TYTHE BARN
SWALCLIFFE
AREA OF ROMANO-BRITISH SETTLEMENT
N
WIGGINTON
SEE MAP 12

CROWN COPYRIGHT RESERVED

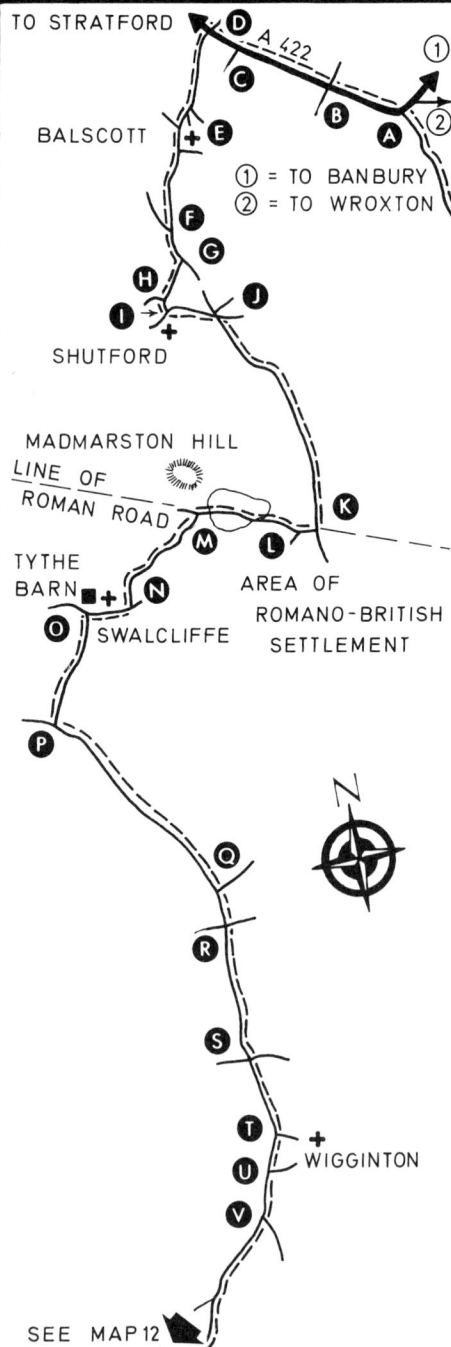

Map REFERENCE	Miles	DIRECTIONS FOR DRIVER	FOLLOW SIGN MARKE
A	1.3	Turn left at T junction on to A 422 (But turn right to visit Wroxton)	Edge Hill
B	.4	Over X rds.	Edge Hill
C	.5	Straight, not left, at T junction	Edge Hill
D	.4	Turn left, off A 422 at X rds.	Balscott
	.5	Enter Balscott, and.....	
E		Fork right (Keep straight through village)	No sign
	.2	Butcher's Arms on right	
F	.6	Straight, not right by sewage works in valley	Shutford
G	.1	Turn right at T junction	Shutford
	.1	Enter Shutford	
H	.1	Fork left, keeping on lower road	No sign
I	.2	Turn sharp left by George & Dragon Inn	North Newington
J	.3	Bear right at five way cross roads	Tadmarto
K	1.3	Turn right at T junction (Now on the course of a Roman Road)	Swalcliffe Lea
L	.1	Fork right	No sign
	.3	Area here was the site of a Romano-British settlement. Madmarston Hill off to right was the site of an Iron Age hill fort	
M	.3	Turn left at T junction (Leaving line of Roman Road)	No sign
	.6	Enter Swalcliffe village	
N	.1	Turn right, on to B 4035	No sign
O	.2	Turn left beyond filling station on left and tithe barn on right (WATCH FOR THIS TURN WITH CARE)	No sign
P	.7	Turn left at T junction by farm	No sign
	.6	'Stour Well' on left. This trough marks the rising of the River Stour	
Q	.7	Straight, not left	No sign
R	.1	Over X rds.	Wigginto
S	.7	Over X rds.	Wigginto
T	.4	Straight, not left Beyond the Swan (But turn left to visit Wigginton)	Great Te
U	.2	Straight, not left	Great Te
V	.3	Fork right	Swerfor
	.7	Fork left	No sign
		Total mileage on this map: 11.9	

PLACES OF INTEREST ON THE ROUTE

Wroxton

Wroxton 'Abbey' is in fact a fine 17th century mansion. It now belongs to an American university, but its delightful gardens and park are open regularly, and well worth visiting. The house's builder, Sir William Pope, lies with his wife in a beautiful canopied tomb in the nearby church. This 14th century building also contains an elegant monument by Flaxman to Lord North, Prime Minister in the reign of George III. Also buried here is Thomas Coutts, founder of that most revered of banking houses.

Wroxton village, with its attractive tree shaded duck pond, is full of thatched stone cottages, so typical of this north Oxfordshire countryside, where the stone is less suitable for splitting into tiles, than it is further to the south and west. Each roofing method has its own merits, but how pleasant these cottages look, with their climbing roses and small gardens.

Balscott

A minute village, undisturbed by the ironstone workings nearby. It consists of a few farms and cottages, a small inn called the Butcher's Arms, and a 14th century church on a small knoll. This has a thin, pinnacled tower, up which one can look from within the porch, with the 'weight' of the church clock hanging immediately above. The interior has been heavily restored.

Shutford

Quiet village amidst small bumpy hills. The prettily signed George and Dragon inn is comfortably sited almost beneath the church. This has a miniature pinnacled tower, Norman arcading, a pleasant oak screen and early 19th century box pews. There is a bridle-path south from here to Swalcliffe.

Madmarston Hill

Site of an Iron Age hill fort. The Roman road at its foot ran from Worcester, through Alcester and Stratford, crossing the Fosse Way at Ettington, and passing Madmarston towards Kings Sutton. Evidence of an extensive Romano-British settlement has been unearthed between the hill and the farm on our left.

Swalcliffe

A most attractive village with a massive Tythe Barn, said to have been built by William of Wykeham (see Broughton, page 21). The Wykeham family have long associations with Swalcliffe, evidence of which may be found in the church. This is a most agreeable building and has been treated with care by the 'restorers'. The roof looks down on pleasing 17th century seating, pulpit and lectern; and colourful tombs of the same period.

Wigginton

Quiet village above the little River Swere, with a church containing several interesting items. See especially the medieval stone seat with a swan at the finial of the arch above it, and also the lovely 15th century roof to the nave.

1. Cottages at Wroxton

2. Shutford Church

3. The road to Swalcliffe

4. House with shell porch, Wigginton

23

MAP 12

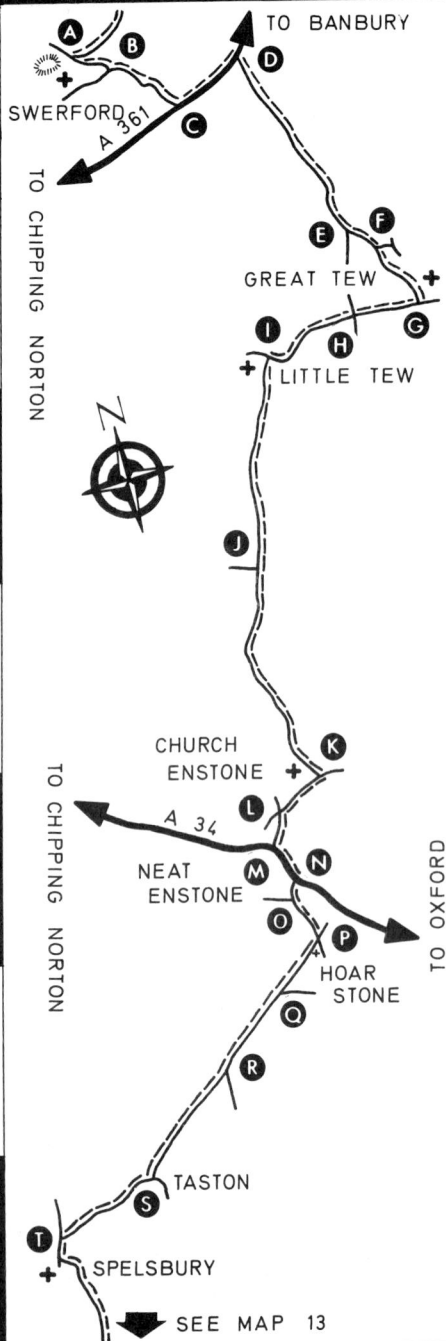

TO BANBURY

SWERFORD A 361

TO CHIPPING NORTON

GREAT TEW

LITTLE TEW

N

CHURCH ENSTONE

A 34

NEAT ENSTONE

TO CHIPPING NORTON

TO OXFORD

HOAR STONE

TASTON

SPELSBURY

SEE MAP 13

Map Reference	Miles	DIRECTIONS FOR DRIVER	FOLLOW SIGN MARKED
A	.6	Bear left at T junction beyond gate, opposite small waterfall, and..... Enter Swerford	No sign
B	.2	Bear left at T junction (But turn right to visit church)	Banbury
C	.5	Turn left, on to A 361	Bloxham
	.2	Mason's Arms on left	
D	.3	Turn right, on to B 4022	The Tews
E	1.1	Fork left and enter Great Tew	Great Tew
F	.2	Fork right by phone box (But fork left for village green, which is well worth a visit)	No sign
	.4	Tew church up avenue on left	
G	.1	Turn right at T junction	Little Tew
H	.4	Over X rds., crossing B 4022	Little Tew
	.3	Enter Little Tew	
I	.1	Turn left at T junction	Enstone
J	1.2	Straight, not right	Enstone
	1.1	Enter Enstone; church on right	
K	.2	Turn right at T junction on to B 4030	No sign
L	.3	Turn left at X rds. opposite entry to Westminster Bank Training College	No sign
M	.2	Turn left on to A 34, with care	No sign
N	.3	Turn right, off A 34, and immediately.....	Fulwell
O	.1	Straight, not right	No sign
P	.3	Turn right at X rds., on to B 4022. Hoar Stone in bushes on south side	Charlbury
Q	.4	Straight, not left	No sign
R	.4	Fork right, off B 4022	Spelsbury
S	.9	Turn right at T junction (Taston Cross down to left)	Spelsbury
T	.6	Turn left at T junction on to B 4026	Charlbury
		Keep on B 4026 through Spelsbury	
		Total mileage on this map: 10.3	

PLACES OF INTEREST ON THE ROUTE

1. The Post Office, Great Tew

Swerford

Has a pleasant green by the church, which is set in a neat churchyard, overlooking the earthworks of a vanished Norman(?) castle, and has a dumpy spire and a 13th century porch with earthy gargoyles.

Great Tew

A 'model' village constructed by the early 19th century landscape gardener, John Loudon, as part of an extensive park overlooking the Worton valley. Hence the unusual number of evergreens in 'Tewland'. There are 'picturesque' stone cottages, an inn and stocks on the village green; but it was planned so long ago, that it no longer appears contrived.

The manor where Lord Falkland entertained poets and philosophers from Oxford, has been replaced by an odd 19th century mansion, built by the descendants of Matthew Boulton, partner of James Watt in the famous Soho Foundry. Great Tew therefore owes its idyllic setting to Black Country sweat in the early years of the Industrial Revolution.

One of the Boultons, Mary, is remembered in the church above the manor where there is a brilliant monument to her by Chantrey. The approach to the church is up a delightful tree lined path, and the attractive interior makes this walk worthwhile.

2. The Hoar Stone

Little Tew

With a Victorian church and a few pleasant houses, Little Tew lies near the source of the River Dorne (see page 19).

Enstone

Church Enstone and Neat Enstone face each other across the valley of the little River Glyme.

Traffic still thunders through Neat Enstone, but happily Church Enstone lies well away from the over-busy A 34. It is prettily sited on slopes above the Glyme valley, with an attractive inn called the Crown, and a little road lined with cottages leading up to the church. This has retained its character well, and is full of interest. See especially the fine Norman south doorway, the 15th century porch and the touching monument to Stevens Wisdom in the south aisle.

3. The Old Cross, Taston

The Hoar Stone

In fact there are three great stones here, the remains of a Stone Age burial chamber. The mound which must have covered the chamber has long since vanished, but the stones are in bushes to the immediate south of the cross roads at Point P.

Taston

Small hamlet with the base of a medieval wayside cross a short distance away from our road.

Spelsbury

An unpretenious village with a pleasant blending of stone and thatch, a row of gabled almshouses and church containing a series of splendid monuments to the Lee family. Do not miss this.

4. Spelsbury Church

5. Tombstone, Spelsbury

25

Map of Charlbury, Ditchley Park, Glympton and Wootton area with route points A–R, Woods, River Glyme, B 4437, A 34, Alternative Route, See Map 14.

Map REFERENCE	Miles	DIRECTIONS FOR DRIVER	FOLLOW SIGN MARKE...
	1.4	Charlbury entry signed	
A		Keep straight into centre of Charlbury	
B	.2	Straight, not right, by the White Hart	Enstone
C		Straight over X rds. by the Rose & Crown	Finstock
D	.6	Bear left on to B 4437 (Keep on this for 2.3 miles)	Woodstoc...
E	2.3	Turn left at small X rds. just before small wood on left WATCH FOR THIS WITH GREAT CARE	No sign
		(NOTE: The road from here to Point F is rather rough in places, although in our view worth the effort. If you wish to avoid it, drive ahead on B 4437 until you reach A 34. Turn left and drive on A 34 to rejoin the route at Point H, where you must turn right for Glympton on to B4027)	
	.9	Ditchley Park (mansion) just visible up avenue to left	
F	.7	Turn right at T junction	No sign
G	.7	Turn right with care on to A 34	Woodstoc...
H	.3	Turn left on to B 4027	Glympto...
	.6	Entrance to Glympton Park on left	
I	.2	Straight, not right	Glympto...
	.1	Enter Glympton and cross River Glyme	
J	.1	Turn right at T junction, keeping on B 4027	Wootto...
K	.9	Straight, not left	Bletchingo...
L	.1	Turn right just beyond the 'Killingworth Castle'	Woottor...
	.1	Enter Wootton	
M	.2	Bear left just before the church	No sigr...
N	.1	Straight, not left	No sigr...
O	.1	Fork left, and immediately fork left again	No sigr...
	.1	Re-cross the River Glyme	
P	.3	Turn left at T junction	Woodsto...
Q	.5	Straight, not left	Woodsto...
R	.1	Almost immediately turn left on to A 34 Total mileage on this map: 10.6	

PLACES OF INTEREST ON THE ROUTE

Charlbury

Small town, tucked away in the Evenlode valley, enviably far from the busy main roads. Charlbury looks across the valley to the 600 acre Cornbury Park, which is backed by the great woodlands of Wychwood Forest. Commuting Oxonians have brought fresh life to Charlbury, but it retains a most agreeable rural flavour, not least in its assortment of appetising inns.

The mainly Perpendicular church is not exceptional, but it blends in well with the stone fronted houses, shops and inns that constitute this pleasant town.

During your exploration of Charlbury (on foot please), do not miss the delightfully elaborate 19th century 'fountain', built to commemorate the visit of Queen Victoria to Charlbury.....a real period piece.

1. *The Bell Hotel, Charlbury*

Ditchley Park

A splendid mansion in a 300 acre park, designed by James Gibbs in 1772, with interior decoration by William Kent. Ditchley was the week-end headquarters of Winston Churchill in the war, and is now an Anglo-American Conference centre. For this reason it is only open to the public for a short period in early August. Enter from Charlbury (turn left at junction C), and re-join route at junction F, by taking the Kiddington exit.

2. *Near Ditchley Park*

Glympton

Here we re-join the lovely Glyme valley, last seen at Enstone. Much money has been spent on this recently built 'Cotswold' village, which is already mellowing satisfactorily. The Glyme tumbles over a small waterfall by the bridge.....a lovely, cool place in high summer.

The church lies behind the great house in lush Glympton Park, and the delightful walk amply justifies a visit. See the splendid tomb of Thomas Teesdale, wool trader and benefactor of Balliol and Pembroke Colleges.

3. *Glympton Park*

Wootton

Attractive village whose steep narrow streets climb up from the bridge over the Glyme. St. Mary's church has a pleasingly plain tower, and a beautiful 13th century south porch.

Why is the inn at Wootton called the Killingworth Castle? It is possible that it was named after Kenilworth Castle, as this unusual spelling has been encountered in several ancient books on Kenilworth. However, it appears that a 17th owner named Killingworth decided to perpetuate his name by changing the title of the inn. In any event, it would be pointless to search for fortifications hereabouts, for there are none.

4. *Wootton village*

27

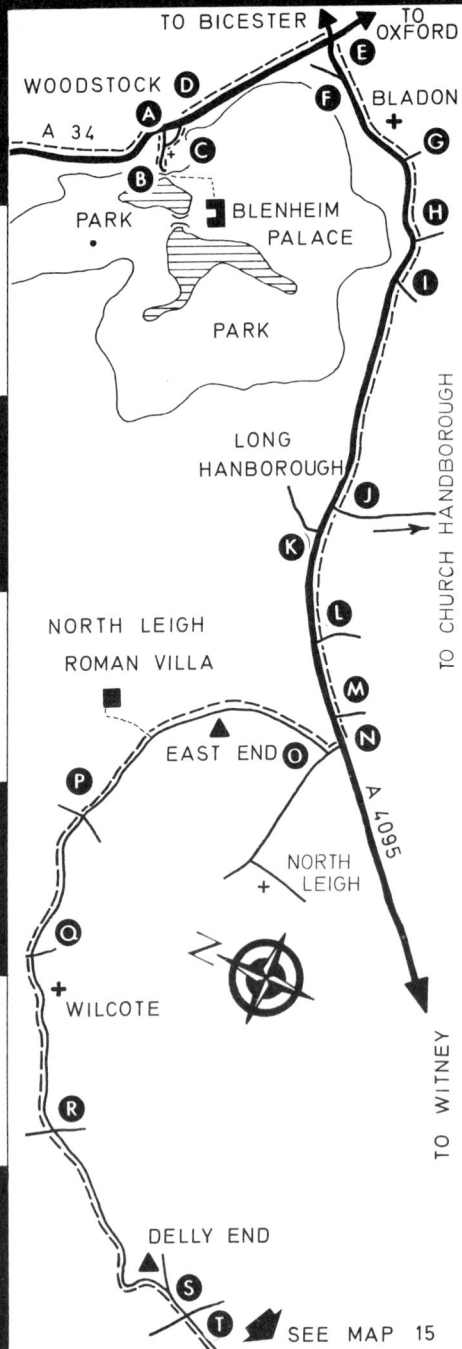

MAP 14

Map Reference	Miles	DIRECTIONS FOR DRIVER	FOLLOW SIGN MARKED
	.5	Enter Woodstock	
A	.8	Turn right in centre, by the King's Arms	'Market Street'
B	.2	Entrance to Blenheim Palace at far end of street. Turn round here	
C	.1	Fork right by Town Hall	No sign
D	.2	Turn right on to A 34	Oxford
E	.9	Turn right at roundabout, on to A 4095	Witney
F	.2	Straight, not right, beyond entry to Bladon (Keep on A 4095 for 4.5 miles)	Bladon
	.6	Bladon church on left	
G	.2	Straight, not left by the Lamb Inn	No sign
H	.4	Straight, not left	Witney
I	.2	Straight, not left	Witney
	.2	Long Hanborough entry signed	
	.5	George and Dragon on right	
J	.5	Straight, not left by the Three Horseshoes (But turn left if you wish to visit Hanborough church..... 1 mile)	Witney
K	.2	Straight, not right	Witney
L	.5	Straight, not left	Witney
M	.5	Straight, not left	Witney
N	.1	Turn right, off A 4095	Finstock
O	.1	Almost immediately turn right again (But go straight ahead and take first turn left if you wish to visit North Leigh church..... 1 mile)	East End
	.6	Through hamlet of East End. Leather Bottle Inn on left	
	.5	Path to North Leigh Roman Villa on right Limited parking space on left	
P	.7	Over X rds.	Wilcote
	.6	Wilcote House over to right	
Q	.2	Over X rds. and between gate posts	Ramsden
	.1	Wilcote Manor on right	
	.1	Wilcote church on left	
R	.8	Over offset X rds.	Delly End
	.5	Straight, not left	No sign
	.5	Enter Delly End	
S	.2	Straight, not left, twice at Delly End green	No sign
T	.1	Over X rds. crossing B 4022	Crawley
		Total mileage on this map: 11.8	

SEE MAP 15

CROWN COPYRIGHT RESERVED

PLACES OF INTEREST ON THE ROUTE

1. 'House with Shutters', Woodstock

Woodstock

Owes its prosperous charm to the kings who had a manor here, to the Churchills, who earned the reward of Blenheim and to the tourists, whose requirements are cared for with a dignity so often lacking in towns of such popularity.

From the main road to the massive park gate, Woodstock has a wonderful assortment of 17th and 18th century houses. The dignified Town Hall was built at the Duke's expense in 1766 and makes a perfect foil for the cosier charms of the Bear Hotel.

The church has a splendid 18th century tower in the Classical style, which belies its interesting medieval interior. Opposite the church is Fletcher's House, which houses the Oxford City and County Museum. This contains a series of displays depicting life and work in Oxfordshire.....very worthwhile.

Blenheim Palace

Once through the entrance gate, one is met by a prospect of palace, bridge and a great lake, with sweeping banks, clad here and there with noble woodlands. This is the work of Vanbrugh and Capability Brown brought to glorious perfection.

Vanbrugh's palace design is magnificent, perhaps a little overwhelming, but the fantastic 2500 acre park has absorbed it effortlessly.

There is far too much to describe here, but amongst all the grandeur, there is the small room where Winston Churchill was born. Also make sure to see the splendid monument to the First Duke and Duchess of Marlborough in the chapel.

2. Blenheim Palace

Bladon

Sir Winston Churchill lies in a simple grave in the churchyard here, only a short distance from the great woodlands bordering Blenheim Park.

Church Hanborough

Small village, with a church which amply justifies our diversion. This has a tall, slender spire, and here are yew trees lining the path to the large north porch, which shelters a fine Norman doorway. The interior, with its old stone floors, is full of character, and there is an interesting 15th century rood screen and a roof of the same period.

3. Bladon Church

North Leigh

The church is situated at the northern end of the village, beside a handsome rectory. See the exceptionally beautiful north aisle chapel, with its fan vaulting and monuments, and the fierce 'doom' wall paintings over the chancel arch.

North Leigh Roman Villa

Situated in the lush Evenlode valley, this site was excavated in 1813, when 60 rooms surrounding a courtyard were revealed. Only one mosaic pavement visible, but this is excellent.

Wilcote

A quiet, tree shaded hamlet, with a small rather uninteresting church.

4. Mosaic Pavement, North Leigh Villa

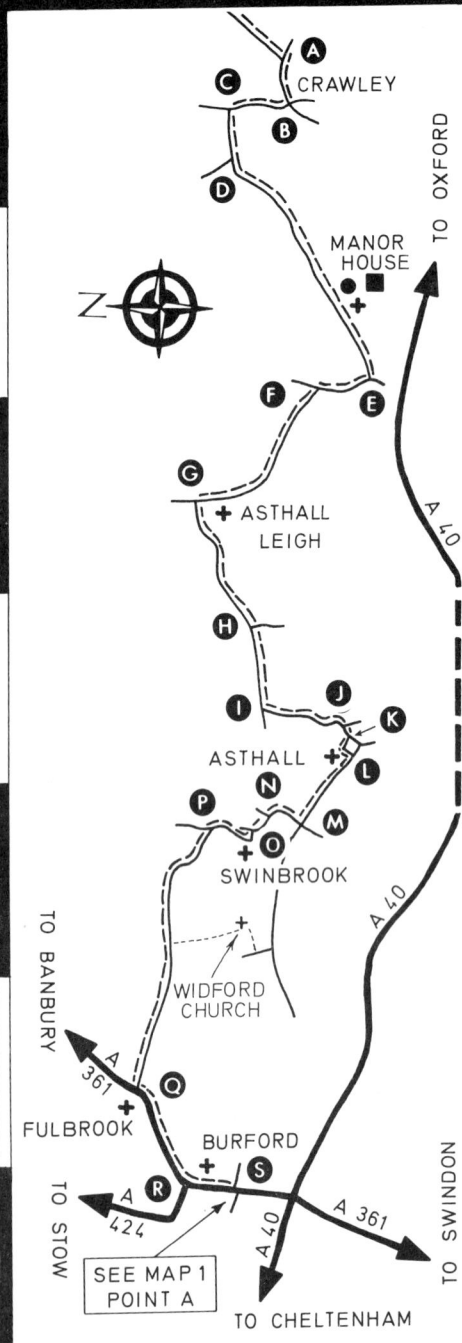

CRAWLEY

A — Manor House — Minster Lovell church and manor ruins

ASTHALL LEIGH

ASTHALL

SWINBROOK

WIDFORD CHURCH

TO OXFORD

TO BANBURY

TO STOW

FULBROOK

BURFORD

A 361

A 424

A 40

TO SWINDON

TO CHELTENHAM

SEE MAP 1 POINT A

N

Map Reference	Miles	DIRECTIONS FOR DRIVER	FOLLOW SIGN MARKED
A	.8	Turn right at T junction and.....	
		Enter Crawley	Crawley
	.1	New Inn on left	
B	.1	Turn right at X rds. by War Memorial, and.....	Minster Lovell
		Lamb Inn on left	
C	.3	Turn left at X rds	Minster Lovell
D	.3	Straight, not right, leaving wider road	Minster Lovell
	.6	Minster Lovell church and manor ruins visible ahead	
	.3	Enter Minster Lovell	
	.3	Straight, not left by small car park for church and manor ruins	No sign
		DO NOT MISS THIS	
E	.2	Turn right beyond the Swan Hotel	No sign
F	.3	Fork left	Asthall Leigh
G	1.0	Turn left by Asthall Leigh church	Asthall
	.1	Old Crown Cottage on left	
H	.6	Straight, not left	Asthall
I	.5	Turn left at T junction	Asthall
	.4	Over bridge crossing the Windrush, and.....	
J		Turn right at entry to Asthall	Swinbrook
K	.1	Bear right by the Three Horseshoes Inn	No sign
	.1	Church on right	
L	.1	Turn right at small T junction	No sign
M	.3	Turn right at X rds. (But go straight ahead and turn right after .5, to visit Widford church)	Swinbrook
	.1	Over Windrush by Swan Inn	
N	.1	Straight, not right at entry to Swinbrook	No sign
O	.2	Church on left	
P	.2	Fork left at top of village	No sign
	.7	Path on left in bottom of valley, leading down to Widford church	
	.6	Dropping down into Fulbrook	
Q	.2	Turn left, on to A 361	Burford
	.1	Straight, not right by War Memorial	No sign
		(But turn right to visit Fulbrook church)	
	.1	Straight, not right, keeping on A 361	No sign
	.1	Carpenter's Arms on left	
R	.2	Bear left, keeping on A 361, at entry to Burford	Swindon
		Over old bridge, crossing Windrush	
	.1	Church up road to left	
S	.2	Arrive Tolsey Museum, Burford, linking on to Map 1, Point A	
		Total mileage on this map: 9.4	

Crawley

Pleasantly sited in valley, with an inn and a few farms and cottages looking down on its small stream.

Minster Lovell

The ruined 15th century manor house of the Lovells is romantically sited on the willow bordered banks of the Windrush. Do not overlook the circular dovecot, nor the fine cruciform church. With its vaulted central crossing. The village itself is perhaps rather self-consciously trim, but it is good to see the buildings so well maintained. There is a delightful little hotel here.....the Old Swan.

1. The Manor House, Minster Lovell

Asthall Leigh

Small upland village looking south across the Windrush valley towards the distant line of the Berkshire Downs. The Old Crown Inn no longer offers refreshment, and is now entitled 'Old Crown Cottage'. The Victorian church appears to be of little interest to visitors.

Asthall

This is one of the classic Windrush villages, complete with water meadows, willow trees, gabled Elizabethan manor overlooking small church, and a tidy little inn. No single item is exceptional, but together they spell perfection.

2. The Old Swan, Minster Lovell

Swinbrook

A delectable village, whose rough sloping green is enlivened by a small stream, and whose church must on no account be passed by. A fine Perpendicular window fills the whole of its east end and light floods in upon two gorgeous 'three-decker' wall tombs in which there are six male members of the Fettiplace family, all lying on their right sides, looking not upwards but outwards. See also the carved medieval chancel stalls.

In the churchyard there is a less splendid, but more poignant memorial.....to Unity Valkyrie Mitford, whose childhood years in Swinbrook are so wonderfully described by her sister Jessica in 'Hons and Rebels'.

3. Fettiplace Monument, Swinbrook

Widford

Walk across a field beyond the Windrush, and below Widford Manor, to visit this delightfully unspoilt little church, with its box pews, 14th century wall paintings, and old stone floor incorporating part of a Roman mosaic pavement.

Fulbrook

Large village astride the A 361, and only separated from Burford by the Windrush and its water-meadows. It has an interesting church just away from the main road. This has a beautiful Norman south doorway, a fine 16th century roof supported on well carved corbel figures, a series of solid 12th century arcade capitals and an opulently colourful 17th century monument in the chancel.

4. The Ford at Swinbrook

INDEX

	Page
Abingdon	11
Akeman Street	3
Appleford	10
Arnold, Matthew	9
Asthall	31
Asthall Leigh	31
Aston	7
Bablock Hythe	9
Bacon, John	17
Baldons, The	13
Balliol College	27
Balscott	23
Bampton	5
Barford St. John	21
Barford St. Michael	21
Barley Mow Inn	13
Barton Abbey	18
Beckley	15
Bladon	29
Blenheim Palace	29
Bletchingdon	17
Bloxham	21
Boulton, Mary	25
Boulton, Matthew	25
Brindley, James	17
Brown, Capability	29
Broughton	21
Broughton Castle	21
Broughton Poggs	5
Burford	3
Chantrey, Sir Francis	25
Charlbury	27
Cherwell, River	16, 19
Church Hanborough	29
Churchill, Sir Winston	27, 29
Clanfield	5
Clifton Hampden	13
Coghill family	17
Cokethorpe Park	7
Cornbury Park	27
Cote	7
Cothill	9
Cottrell-Dormer family	19
Coutts, Thomas	23
Crawley	31
Cripps, Sir Stafford	5
Cumnor	9
Daylesford	7
Day's Lock	13
Deloraine, Lord	19
Delly End	28
Didcot	10
Ditchley Park	27
Dorchester	13
Dorne, River	19, 25
Drayton	11
Dry Sandford	9
Dunch family	13
East End	28
Eastleach Martin	3
Eastleach Turville	3
Edward the Confessor	17
Enstone	25
Evenlode, River	25, 27, 29
Eynsham	9
Eynsham Abbey	9, 15
Falkland, Lord	25
Farmoor Reservoir	9
Fettiplace family	3
Filkins	5
Flaxman, John	23
Fletcher's House	29
Forest Hill	15
Forster, Anthony	9
Fulbrook	31
Garsington	13
Gibbs, James	27
Glyme, River	25, 27
Glympton	27
Glympton Park	27
Hampton Gay	17
Harborne, John	17
Harcourt family	7
Harcourt, Lord	7
Hastings, Warren	7
Hoar Stone	25
Hopcroft's Holt	19
Islip	17
Kempster, Christopher	11
Kent, William	19, 27
Kiddington	27
Killingworth Castle, The	27
Langford	5
Leach, River	3
Leicester Earl of	9
Lenthall, Speaker	3
Long Hanborough	28
Loudon, John	25
Lovell family	31
Madmarston Hill	23
Marlborough, Duke of	29
Marsh Baldon	13
Middle Barton	19
Milton, John	15
Minster Lovell	31
Mitford, Unity	31
Mitford, Jessica	31
Monmouth, Duke of	19
Nether Worton	19
New College	15, 21
North, Lord	23
North Leigh	29
North Leigh Roman Villa	29
Otmoor	15
Over Worton	19
Oxford Canal	17
Oxford County Museum	29
Pembroke College	27
Pendon Museum	13
Pinkhill Lock	9
Pope, Alexander	7
Pope, Sir William	23
Pope's Tower	7
Powell, Mary	15
Ray, River	17
Rock of Gibraltar Inn	16
Robsart, Amy	9
Rousham Park & village	19
Sandford Park	19
Sandford St. Martin	19
Saye & Sele, Lord	21
Scott, Sir Gilbert	13
Shutford	23
Sinodun Hills	13
Soar, River	20
Soho Foundry	25
Spelsbury	25
Stanton Harcourt	7
Stanton St. John	15
Steeple Barton	19
Street, G.E.	5, 15, 21
Sutton Courtenay	11
Sutton Pool	11
Swalcliffe	23
Swere, River	21, 25
Swerford	25
Swinbrook	31
Swinford Bridge	9